Pants on Fire

Poems by
Paul Cookson

Illustrated by
David Parkins

MACMILLAN CHILDREN'S BOOKS

Dedicated to Bob Hartman,
great storyteller, great inspiration and great friend

First published 2005 by Macmillan Children's Books
a division of Macmillan Publishers Limited
20 New Wharf Road, London N1 9RR
Basingstoke and Oxford
www.panmacmillan.com

Associated companies throughout the world

ISBN-13: 978-0-330-41798-3
ISBN-10: 0-330-41798-3

Text copyright © Paul Cookson 2005
Illustrations copyright © David Parkins 2005

The right of Paul Cookson and David Parkins to be identified as the
author and illustrator of this work has been asserted by them in
accordance with the Copyright, Designs and Patents Act 1988.

3 5 7 9 8 6 4

A CIP catalogue record for this book is available from
the British Library.

Printed and bound in Great Britain by Mackays of Chatham plc, Kent

Contents

First and Lasting Impressions

I want to be

the first shadow dancing in the sunrise
the last negative ghost that lengthens into darkness

the first footprint crump on the blank and silent snowy canvas
the last drop that melts disappearing into sunlight

the first explosive splash shattering the mirrored pool
the last slowing ripple ironed into calmness

the first track followed on the ocean-swept sand
the last print washed into watery oblivion

Pants on Fire

I can change a tractor tyre
Visit Hobbits in the shire
Balance high upon a wire
Liar, liar! Pants on fire!
Liar, liar! Pants on fire!

I can't stand this heating
Driving me insane
Wherever I am seating
My bottom is in pain
Feel the flames reaching higher
Ooh! Aah! Pants on fire!
Ooh! Aah! Pants on fire!

Pants on fire! Pants on fire!
Liar, liar! Pants on fire!

I can climb the highest spire
Sing in tune in the choir
Bite the neck of a big vampire
Liar, liar! Pants on fire!
Liar, liar! Pants on fire!

I am always fuming
Butt it is no joke
Big black clouds ballooning
Swirling plumes of smoke
Glowing in this strange attire
Ooh! Aah! Pants on fire!
Ooh! Aah! Pants on fire!

Pants on fire! Pants on fire!
Liar, liar! Pants on fire!

Always in the hot seat
Wherever I am going
The scorching and the torching
My rear is always glowing
Hotter than a deep-fat fryer
Glowing in this strange attire
Feel the flames reaching higher
Ooh! Aah! Pants on fire!

Pants on fire! Pants on fire!
Liar, liar! Pants on fire!

My Football Counting Rhyme

I kicked my football
Once against the wall
Twice in the bathroom
Three times in the hall

Four times in the kitchen
Five times at the door
Six at my sister
Then seven more

Eight against the gate
Nine against the slide
Ten against the greenhouse
And then I had to hide!

Going Nowhere Fast

Roadworks
Delays Expected Until September

On the motorway, in the passenger seat,
I look at my watch . . .
Ten past three on the twenty-sixth of March.
And we could be here till September?
That's five, no six months!
We haven't brought any sandwiches.
No telly.
No toilet.
No nothing.
Just cars. And cars.
And lorries. And caravans. And more cars.
As the traffic grinds to a juddering halt
So does my heart as time stands still
And we start going nowhere . . .
Fast.

These Are the Hands

These are the hands that wave
These are the hands that clap
These are the hands that pray
These are the hands that tap

These are the hands that grip
These are the hands that write
These are the hands that paint
These are the hands that fight

These are the hands that hug
These are the hands that squeeze
These are the hands that point
These are the hands that tease

These are the hands that fix
These are the hands that mend
These are the hands that give
These are the hands that lend

These are the hands that take
These are the hands that poke
These are the hands that heal
These are the hands that stroke

These are the hands that hold
These are the hands that love
These are the hands of mine
That fit me like a glove

Full of Surprises

This poem is full of surprises
Each line holds something new
This poem is full of surprises
Especially for you . . .

It's full of tigers roaring
It's full of loud guitars
It's full of comets soaring
It's full of shooting stars

It's full of pirates fighting
It's full of winning goals
It's full of alien sightings
It's full of rock and roll

It's full of rainbows beaming
It's full of eagles flying
It's full of dreamers dreaming
It's full of teardrops drying

It's full of magic spells
It's full of wizards' pointy hats
It's full of fairy elves
It's full of witches and black cats

It's full of dragons breathing fire
It's full of dinosaurs
It's full of mountains reaching higher
It's full of warm applause

It's full of everything you need
It's full of more besides
It's full of food, the world to feed
It's full of fairground rides

It's full of love and happiness
It's full of dreams come true
It's full of things that are the best
Especially for you

It's jammed and crammed and packed and stacked
With things both old and new
This poem is full of surprises
Especially for you.

Rejected Names Found in a Superhero's Bin

Quite Good Bloke

Thoroughly Decent Excellent Chap

Terrific Kinda Guy

Out-Of-This-World Fellow

Incomparable Glorious Dude

Wonderful Smashing Sensational Person

Anytime Anyplace Anywhere Man

I-Might-Be-Able-To-Make-It-Every-Second-Thursday Boy

Flyfast Goodfighter

Brickjaw Mighty Fist

The Pink Defender

Judge Fred

Hat Man

The Silver Server

Soupy Man

Captain Retford

11

A Sumo Wrestler Chappy

A sumo wrestler chappy
One day in the ring was unhappy
When thrown to the ground
His mum pinned him down
And in view of the crowd changed his nappy.

Haiku Boy

Danger? No problem
I save the world e-ve-ry
Seventeen seconds

Nearly Heroes

Papergirl just folded
Jellyboy just set
Geographyman got lost
We haven't found him yet

Fireboy went out
Appleman went rotten
The memorable Thingumajig-girl
Is easily forgotten

Dinghywoman burst
Dietgirl just faded
Balloonboy just drifted
Lackadaisicalgirl is jaded

Frostman melted away
Ostrichman had his head in the sand
The Shadow is scared of the dark
Designboy has got nothing planned

Codgirl has been battered
Torchman has gone dim
Lumberjackbloke has got the chop
Reaperman is grim

Nonplussedman cannot be bothered
Indifferentgirl lives up to her name
Lethargicboy and Listlesslady
They're both just the same

Electricboy has blown a fuse
Generatorgirl just can't get going
Middleagedman is past it
And Cheap-pun-man wrote this poem

The Martial Art of Marshall Hart

Frizzy hair and four-foot six
A forest of freckles and a zillion zits
Permanently dazzled, permanently dazed
Milk-bottle specs, double-glazed
Once seen, soon forgotten
Muscles just like knots in cotton
An obvious target, a natural victim
Sick that the big boys always picked him
They'd bend his specs, spit on his chips
Play dot-to-dot with his spots and zits
Steal his homework, call him a freak
Every single day of the week
Rough, tough, smug and smart
Until enough was enough for Marshall Hart

Evening classes every night
Self-defence and how to fight
Ju-jitsu and tae kwon do
T'ai chi, judo and kung fu
Toned his body and trained his brain
Harnessed the power and took the strain

The white pyjamas, and art of Zen
Practised again and again and again
No longer a mouse, nearly a man
A frizzy, dizzy Jackie Chan
A shadow of the kid he used to be
A freckled, spectacled Bruce Lee
Straight as an arrow, fast as a dart
Better watch out for Marshall Hart

Belts changed quickly, yellow to black
Self-defence turned to attack
Frontflip backflip acrobatics
Slow-mo somersault dramatics
A ginger ninja ballerina
Grace and poise but lean and meaner
Super slick and lightning quick
Rabbit kick – neat trick
Denting doors with a swift headbutt
Snapping planks with a kick from his foot
Pushing a car and pulling a wagon
Exit the wimp, enter the dragon
Karate-chopping bricks apart
There's no stopping Marshall Hart

Cool and calm he looks the part
No one's able to outsmart
Or upset the applecart
He's a walking work of art
Just one word and he will start
Pummelling personal private parts
Squashing noses like jam tarts
Now no one messes, no one starts
With the martial art of Marshall Hart

Uncle John's Legs

It isn't the things that go bump in the night
It isn't the venom from Dracula's bite
It isn't the shadows that give me a fright
It's Uncle John's legs – all ghostly and white.

It isn't the howl of the wolf at the moon
It isn't the monster from the lagoon
It isn't the glow of green bones in the gloom
It's Uncle John's legs that fill me with doom.

Unspeakably spindly, all ghoulish and glowing
Bubbling and bulgy blue blood vessels showing
Uncle John's legs keep to-ing and fro-ing
Following me wherever I'm going

They infest my nightmares when I'm in my bed
Their echoing footsteps repeat in my head
But the strange thing is this . . . my Uncle John's dead
Yet I'm followed round by Uncle John's legs
Nobody at all . . . just

Uncle
John's
. . . legs

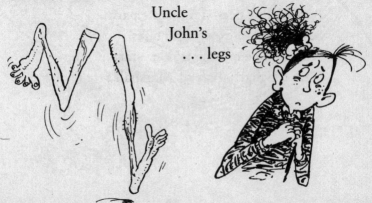

Dread

It's not the flapping skin
It's not the bony fingers
It's not the vice-like squeeze
It's not the rasping breath

Worse than a monster, worse than a ghost
This is what I dread the most . . .

The brush of wiry hairs
The wart upon the lip
Of my great-great-gran
When she kisses me to death!

New Poem

This poem is new
Brand spanking new
Each letter straight from the pen
Each word shiny and polished
Each line freshly forged by the poet.

This poem is new
Brand spanking new
Not worn with over-reading
Not familiar or predictable
It needs to be concentrated on
Because it is new,
Anything could happen . . .
But doesn't

All the words in this poem
May well have been used before
In other poems
But not in this order
For this is a new poem.

A brand-new poem.

A Tall Story

I'm sorry about my report from
St Goliath's School for Trainee Giants.

It's just that I don't think I'm cut out for this life.
For one thing, I'm only three-foot six.

I can't spell 'Beenstork'
And I get mixed up with me 'Feefis' and my 'Fofums'

Smelling blood – especially that of English males
Gives me migraines and sickness

Bone grinding makes me queasy
And I don't like bread.

Plus some of the big lads pick on me.

I'm not making excuses but
I don't think it's all my fault.

I mean
You really shouldn't have called me
Jack

Dear Head Teacher . . .

I'm writing to say sorry about your window that was smashed
It wasn't me that did it, but someone from my class

I didn't kick the ball at all, I didn't really know
I didn't see the shot that took it through your new window . . .

I wasn't even playing, I just happened to be standing
I didn't have a clue where the ball would end up landing

I wasn't really looking, my eyes were closed instead
It wasn't my fault that the ball bounced off my head

If it hadn't hit my head it would just have hit the wall
But you're the one who told me to be standing there at all

Everybody laughed at the ricochet deflection,
Well . . . everyone but me when the football changed direction

Everyone said 'Smashing!' and 'Look what a beauty!'
But it wasn't my fault, I was just on playground duty.

Don't Get Your Knickers in a Twist!

We never knew that Mum could be a great contortionist
Until the underwear she wore decided to resist
She aimed straight for the leg holes but somehow they missed . . .
In a spot, the day she got her knickers in a twist.

They restricted and constricted her like an iron fist
Held hostage by the tightening elastic terrorist
With one leg round her head and the other near her wrist
A human knot, the day she got her knickers in a twist.

She struggled, strained and wrestled but they would not desist
The wrangling and the strangling continued to persist
Walking like an alien exhibitionist
A hop, a squat, a trot, she's got her knickers in a twist.

Trussed up like a chicken, peering through her legs she hissed
'Help me quick! What I need's a physiotherapist!'
Dad didn't seem to understand cos all he said was this . . .
'Keep your hair on, do not fret
There's no need to panic yet
Play it cool, just don't get . . . your knickers in a twist.'

Epitaph for the Last Martian

Crash-landing caused extinction
For the last of the Martian species
Here and here . . . and here and here
He rests in pieces.

Elephants' Graveyard

When the sun is setting on their lives
Their long day fades to dusk
This is their final resting place
Girth to girth, tusk to tusk.

Two Dinosaur Epitaphs

Alive and well no longer
The mighty Brontosaurus
Exit to extinction
The dead-and-gone-to-saurus.

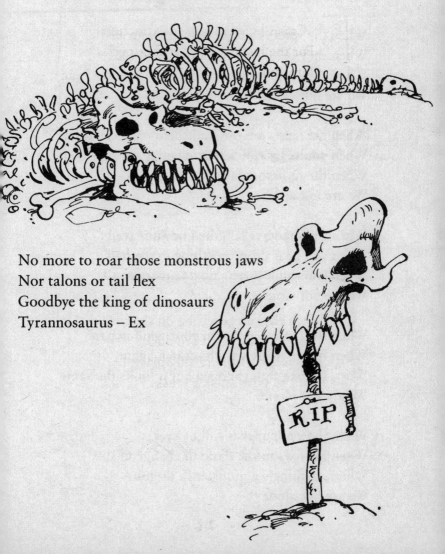

No more to roar those monstrous jaws
Nor talons or tail flex
Goodbye the king of dinosaurs
Tyrannosaurus – Ex

We Are Not Alone

When floorboards creak and hinges squeak
When the TV's off but seems to speak
When the moon is full and you hear a shriek
We are not alone.

When the spiders gather beneath your bed
When they colonize the garden shed
When they spin their webs right above your head
We are not alone.

When the lights are out and there's no one home
When you're by yourself and you're on your own
When the radiators bubble and groan
We are not alone.

When the shadows lengthen on your wall
When you hear deep breathing in the hall
When you think there's no one there at all
We are not alone.

When the branches tap on your windowpane
When finger twigs scritch scratch again
When something's changed but it looks the same
We are not alone.

When the wallpaper is full of eyes
When the toys in the dark all change in size
When anything's a monster in disguise
We are not alone.

You'd better watch out whatever you do
There's something out there looking at you
When you think you are on your own
We are not
We are not
We are not alone.

With You, Without You

With you I'm one of the fearless two
Without you I'm the cautious one.

With you I think I'm the queen of the dance floor
Without you I'm just a clumsy ugly sister.

With you my name is complete
Without you it's just waiting for the 'and'.

With you I feel a hundred per cent
Without you I'm less than fifty.

With you I can take on the world
Without you I just wish you were here.

With you I know that you feel the same
Without you I know that you feel the same.

With you, without you
We are the perfect team.

May You Always

May your smile be ever present
May your skies be always blue
May your path be ever onward
May your heart be ever true

May your dreams be full to bursting
May your steps be always sure
May the fire within your soul
Blaze on for evermore

May you live to meet ambition
May you strive to pass each test
May you find the love your life deserves
May you always have the best

May your happiness be plentiful
May your regrets be few
May you always be my best friend
May you always . . . just be you

Whatevvaaa . . . (Let's All Do the Drama Queen)

Whatevvaaa . . .
Whatevvaaa . . .
Talk to the hand – the face ain't listening
Talk to the hand – the face ain't listening

Girls are superior
Boys are inferior
Girls are superior
Boys are inferior

I'm giving off that look
I'm gonna roll my eyes
I'm gonna shake my head
Breathe loud dramatic sighs

I'm looking down my nose
I'm pursing up my lips
I'm playing with my hair
My hands are on my hips

Whatevvaaa . . .
Whatevvaaa . . .
Talk to the hand – the face ain't listening
Talk to the hand – the face ain't listening

You think I'm doing that
It's sooo not cool
I'm not doing that
I'm no fool

Whatevvaaa . . .
Whatevvaaa . . .
Talk to the hand – the face ain't listening
Talk to the hand – the face ain't listening

I'm so grown up, the coolest on the scene
So grown up, nearly in my teens
So mature, know what I mean
So don't look at me, I'm no drama queen
I'm no drama queen
Don't ignore me, I'm no drama queen

Whatevvaaa . . .
Whatevvaaa . . .
Talk to the hand – the face ain't listening
Talk to the hand – the face ain't listening

Feet and Seasons

The crunch crunch crunch of crispy leaves
The squelch squelch squelch in mud and snow
The tiptoed care through bluebell beds
The warmth of the beach on my bare toes

Stormy-promise Haiku

The rainbow after,
God's graffiti does make it
Easy to believe

You Get On My Nerves

You get on my nerves
You're a pain in the neck
You drive me to distraction

You can't keep secrets
You don't shut up
That's part of the attraction

You see you are
Just like me
One after my own heart

You're my best friend
And that is why
I hate it when we are apart

Six Unlucky Thirteens

A Thirteen is a three-line poem with
thirteen syllables in a 4–5–4 pattern

Threw a black cat
Over my shoulder
Broke a mirror

Not so lucky
Horseshoe broke my toes
Still on the horse

Walked round ladder
Dislocated hip
Tripped on black cat

Friday thirteenth
Full moon, Halloween
Midnight . . . who's there?

Stuck inside house
New umbrella up
Won't fit through door

Whoops! Seven years
Should not have broken
Mirror on Dad

Unsuccessful Monsters

The Look-nice Monster – *there's a welcome in the hillsides*
The Amenable Snowman – *so nice in the ice*
Littlefoot – *never treads on your toes*
The Werewool – *all cuddly and nice*

The Purse of the Mummy – *will buy you a treat*
Cycletops – *lets you ride his bike*
The Vantyre – *always gives you a lift*
Muduser – *gets you as dirty as you like*

What We'd Really Like to Do on Holiday — a Family Poem

Swim and surf and splash and swim and slide and splash
   and swim
Wander round a stately home for an hour or two
Roller coasters, helter-skelters, big dippers, speedway
Walk up a hill and admire the lovely view

Bumper cars, waltzers, big wheels, ghost trains
Find an old museum and artistic gallery
Go-karts, trampolines, crazy golf, climbing frames
Sit down for a while with a nice cream tea

Arcades, slot machines, loud music, flashing lights
Look in all the quaint shops at paintings and antiques
Log flumes, motor boats, waterskis and water fights
Relax with a book on a nice deserted beach

Candyfloss and ice creams, lollies, rock and sticky sweets
A five-course meal for two that takes at least three hours
Hot dogs, fish and chips, doughnuts and burgers
Ornamental gardens sniffing all the flowers

Pony rides, donkey rides, quad bikes and mountain bikes
Inspect the architecture in the older part of town
Roller skating, rollerblading, ice skates and skateboards
Walk around cathedrals, not making a sound

Raves and discos, dancing and laser quest
Have a little picnic where no one is around
Cinemas and videos, karaoke talent shows
Spend hours at a medieval burial ground

Come on, Mum! Come on, Dad! There's loads and loads
    to do!
What we need's a holiday, a holiday from you!
Mum! Dad! Let's chill out and go somewhere dead cool . . .
You can go to Iceland and we'll stay by the pool.

My Rocket

My rocket dreamed of circling the earth,
orbiting the moon,
zigzagging the planets,
looping-the-loop with satellites,
dodging meteorites,
racing comets
and disappearing into time warps and black holes.

Instead, it circled the garden shed,
orbited the swing,
zigzagged the apple tree,
looped-the-loop with the clothes line,
dodged two butterflies,
raced one wasp and a bluebottle
then disappeared over the hedge
into the time warp and black hole
that is Mister Hislop's garden.

Fairground Attraction

I knew she was the one for me
The moment I saw her

My heart looped-the-loop
And helter-skeltered ever faster

But I was like the coconut.
Shy.

High-rise King-size Super-duper Snack

King-prawn mushroom bacon double-cheddar
Chargrilled fish-filled chicken double-header
Marmalade marinade A-grade beef
Toffee-coated nut-brittle crunchy on the teeth.

Triple-decker pickled pepper griddled rack of rib
Battered wedge curried veg peanut satay dip
Deep-filled flame-grilled meat meat meat
Between big bread buns – a tangy tasty treat.

The bigger and the beefier the burger is the better
A fast-food snack-attack appetite whetter
A jack-'em-up pack-'em-up rack-'em-up stack
A high-rise king-size super-duper snack.

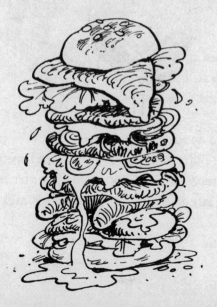

Fair's Fair

I've got . . .
a train set, a Scalextric and a PlayStation
but I never get to play on them.

Dad's always on them,
says he needs to know they work
so he can help me play with them properly.

That was ages ago now
and he's still practising.
I never get to go on them.

What he doesn't know is that
his golf clubs make great swords and spears,
his old records and CDs are brilliant frisbees
and his guitar is a pretty good tennis racket.

Fair's fair

Stardust Dreams

At night
when the sky is clear
I sit and try to count the stars
dreaming upon every one I number.

Very soon I've lost count
but hey, sixty-seven dreams are sixty-seven dreams
and if just one of them should happen to come true
that would be just fine.

There Was a Young Man from Penzance

There was a young man from Penzance
Who kept fourteen-thousand pet ants
They wriggled and itched
He wigged and twitched
Cos he kept all the ants in his pants.

Short Visit, Long Stay

Our school trip was a special occasion
But we never reached our destination
Instead of the zoo
I was locked in the loo
In an M62 service station.

Creation

God, smiling and chuckling
at His own designs.

Knee-deep in feathers and scales,
bits of beak and bone.

Elbows splattered with mud and sand,
clay and water, hair and fur.

Not so much the initial designs that impress,
original though they are.

It's what He did with the leftovers
that's real creative genius.

How else would you get an armadillo
or a duck-billed platypus?

Stepmother

Life with her is a fairy tale
She's not like any other
Totally ace and magically cool
My wicked stepmother.

Gerri the Gerbil's Workout Programme

Beginners:

Round and round the wheel
Round and round the wheel

Intermediate:

Round and round the wheel
Round and round the wheel
Round and round the wheel
Round and round and round the wheel

Competent:

Round and round the wheel
Round and round the wheel
Round and round the wheel
Round and round and round the wheel
Up the stairs
Down the stairs
Round and round the wheel

Advanced:

Round and round the wheel
Round and round the wheel
Round and round the wheel
Round and round and round the wheel
Up the stairs
Down the stairs
In the plastic tube
1 – 2 – 3 – 4 –
Through the plastic tube
Up the stairs
Down the stairs
Round and round the wheel

The Haiku Monster

The haiku monster
Gobbles up the syllables
Crunching words and CHOMP!

The haiku monster
Slurps the 's' in _paghetti
Bites 'b's for _reakfast

The haiku monster
Jumbles all the telrets pu
Makes word disappear.

The haiku monster
Nibbles on the v_w_ls _nd
Chews consonants u_.

The haiku monster
Alphabet joker, plays with
The lettuce and worms.

The haiku monster
Hides rude words in the poem
And spoils *bum snog vest*.

Mixes up the lines
The haiku monster
Ruining all the layout.

The Big Shed

A ramshackle den of clutter,
A mazy mixture of the useful and the useless,
The rubbish and the rusty, wood and mud.

At least three small sheds' worth
Of tongue and groove and four by two,
Dismantled and flat-packed . . . well, sort of . . .
All jumbled zigzag see-saw heaps.

The monster orange rotavator,
Its giant teeth caked with mud,
Silent and untamed –
I was never allowed to grapple this beast
Until I was at secondary school.

The dead red-and-white motor scooter
Complete with windshield and crash helmet
That dad could never get to work
But cousin Paul took and resurrected.

Stacks and stacks and stacks
Of multi-purpose bamboo canes
That would become arrows, guns or swords
Depending on last night's television.

Hay-bales, musty, dusty and precarious
Transformed into forts, mountains or sheer rock faces.

The bowed wooden barrel we broke
One summer-holiday afternoon
When trying to walk inside it, over our heads
Re-enacting an adventure from *Scooby-Doo*.

The legend of 'Hairy Face'
Created then extended
From nothing to belief
Thanks to invented sightings and pretend happenings
All scratching, creakings and whistlings became his.
No one really believed
Until they were left alone at dusk
When darkness extended its bony fingers,
Squeezing out remaining light
And 'Hairy Face' lurked in every single shadow.

Hide-and-seek became a game
With endless possibilities.
No two games identical, our options knew few limits
As plastic sheets, piles of planks,
Pallets and potato sacks
Chimney pots and high haystacks
Were rearranged so that the youthful bodies were
concealed that little bit longer.

We could lose ourselves for hours
In this ramshackle den of clutter,
That mazy mixture of the rubbish and the rusty
The wood, the mud, the useful, the useless
And us.

Three-minute Silence,
Three-minute Poem

bells chime
14th September
2001

all alone in a staffroom in Barnsley
but thinking of America,
remembering New York . . .

the blur of crashing planes as missiles
falling skyscrapers
raging fire and monstrous dust-clouds

and the dead
the innocent dead
the thousands of innocent dead

and still there is the disbelief
numbed with the knowledge of reality
but chilled with disbelief

trying to believe the unbelievable
trying to think of something
just something

half-formed prayers disintegrate
and a half-formed poem
drifts off into nothingness

bells chime
14th September
2001

all alone in a staffroom in Barnsley

Alien Catchphrases

As plain as the face on my nose
My tongue has got the cat
By the teeth of my skin I'm all ears
Heels overhead and mad as a hat.

My flesh creeps warts and all
Three heads are better than one
I feed my hand that bites
I suck the blood from stones

There is a pit in my sinking-feeling stomach
My limit is beyond the sky
Have a heart-to-heart-to-heart with me
And we'll see eye to eye to eye to eye to eye to eye to eye . . .

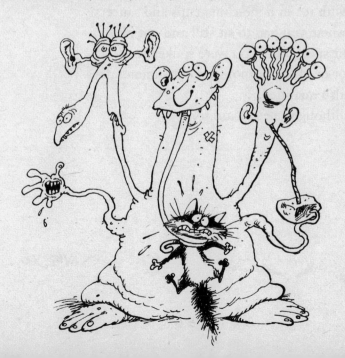

Watching Nails Go Rusty

We seemed to do a lot of it
when I was a child.
At least that's what Dad said it was like
when it took me ages to get a job done
or longer than usual to get ready for church.

The test match on a slow day,
an uneventful England international football match
or waiting for the rain to stop on holiday
would also fit this category.

Personally speaking,
visiting aged female relatives
in old-fashioned houses
with tea in bone-china cups and saucers
where you had to sit still and not play
or speak until you were spoken to,
or overlong sermons on hot summer days
also qualified,
although I never said so.

Yes, we used to do a lot of it then,
watching nails go rusty.
That, and paint drying.
Sometimes we'd do it till the cows came home.

Keep Your Hair, Ron!

Ron's wig cost a million pounds
I suppose that you could say
On Monday what he brought was
A high-price toupee

When Tuesday's whirlwind blew it off
All it brought was sorrow
For what he didn't know on Monday was . . .
Hair today gone tomorrow

Grandad's Garden Shed

The door is always locked
The window's always blocked
The warning sign is propped
With letters bold and red
DANGER! and BEWARE!
KEEP OUT! DON'T YOU DARE!
So what goes on in there . . .
In Grandad's garden shed?

There's banging and there's crashing
There's clanging and there's smashing
There's grinding and there's gnashing
As lights flash overhead
There's growling and there's groaning
There's howling and there's moaning
I'm glad I'm not alone in
Grandad's garden shed.

It's only once a month, when
The moon is bright and full, then
Grandad disappears in
When we're tucked up in bed
No one must go near him
He knows that I can hear him
Nobody must peer in
Grandad's garden shed.

It's strange but it is true
We don't know what to do
Cos Gran is in there too
As well as Uncle Fred,
Mum and Dad and Auntie Flo
Stay there for a week or so
There's something weird that I don't knooooooww . . .
In Grandad's garden shed.

Haik-ewe

Sheep in the distance
Are small clouds on the hillside
Nimbus flocks and flecks

Samson, Samson

Samson, Samson
Big and strong and handsome
His mother's precious son
And his grandmother's grandson

He could kill a lion
With his bare hands on
The beast and knock it off
The ground that it stands on

If you were a Philistine
You wouldn't take a chance on
Getting in a barney
With someone like Samson

Hairy, scary
You'd better be wary
The red mist falls
And he's no fairy

A donkey's jawbone
Swinging and some
Philistines died
That was the plan – son

Samson, Samson
Big and strong and handsome
Along came Delilah
Big romance on

Love is binding
She put her trance on
Poor old Samson
Couldn't keep his pants on

Delilah, Delilah
A liar and beguiler
Teasing out his secrets
Smiling all the whiler

Giving him a haircut
For a ransom
Caught by the Philistines
Poor old Samson

Tortured, blinded
Couldn't even glance on
The jeering and the cheering
The singing and dancing

One last effort
Leaning on a stanchion
Bringing down the house
On the Philistine mansion

Samson, Samson
Big and strong and handsome
All in a poem
With terrible scansion

Twenty Teachers at Our School

The music teacher with no rhythm – Mister Beat

The English teacher who gets things wrong – Miss Take

The depressing French teacher – Miss Eree

Miss Eree

The supply teacher who teaches all subjects – Miss Ellaneous

The exotic dance teacher – Ms Merizing

The PE teacher who cannot score a goal – Mister Nother-penalty

The Geography teacher – Miss Issippi

The teacher nobody knows – Mister E.

Mister E.

The teacher no one understands
– Mister Fy

The drama teacher –
Ms Kerade

Two religious studies teachers –
Miss Belief and Ms Iyah

The very attractive student
teacher who everyone wants to
kiss – Miss Eltoe

Ms Kerade

The outdoor-pursuits teachers
who were once stuck on a desert
island – Miss Adventure and
Miss Age-in-a-bottle

The Italian teacher troubled by
insect bites – Miss Quito

The CDT teacher no one really
knows anything about apart
from the fact that she's good
with wood – Miss Teak

Miss Quito

The music teacher who writes
choruses for competitions never
knowing what he may win –
Mister Reprise

The Greek teacher who looks
like Medusa but instead of
snakes she has feathers –
Miss Tickle-beast

Professor Pinnion

The head of science who
always speaks his mind –
Professor Pinnion

Beware of The Grey

Beware of The Grey
Beware of The Grey
Fading your dreams
And ambitions away

Beware of The Grey
Beware of The Grey
Melting the night-time
Into the day

He'll take all the colours
And drain them away
Beware of the evil
Beware of The Grey

Whatever you do
Whatever you say
Keep your eyes open
Beware of The Grey

Don't put off till tomorrow
What can be done today
Follow your vision
Beware of The Grey

He'll shade all your dreams
And whisper and say
Don't worry, give up
Beware of The Grey

Where there's a will
There's always a way
Little by little
Beware of The Grey

He'll suck out your energy
Say it's OK
To accept second best
Beware of The Grey

Beware of The Grey
Beware of The Grey
Fading your dreams
And ambitions a
                      w
                         a
                            y . . .

Revenge of the Fly

One day during breakfast,
Bacon, ham and eggs,
A little fly buzzed down upon
The top of Billy's head.
Its little furry feet tickled
Across young Billy's brow
And then it flew away
And he thought, 'It's OK now . . .'
He cut a piece of bacon,
Looking forward to its taste,
Was just about to munch it up
And then – across his face
He felt a little tickle
As the fly came in to land . . .
The bacon was uneaten
As the fork fell from his hand.
He shook his head and waved his arms
Up, down and side to side
But the little fly just held on tight
No matter what he tried.
Just then the little fly buzzed off
And Billy, with an evil grin, said,
'For sure that little monster's dead
When it comes back again!'
He found a rolled-up newspaper,
A tea towel and a shoe.
He lay in wait, his breakfast – bait
And knew what he would do.

He heard a little buzzing noise
And then he heard it stop.
Creeping out, with a shout,
He let the towel drop.
Armed with a shoe and paper
He laughed above the plate,
The fly beneath the towel
Would, could not escape.
He brought the paper flying down
With a squelchy, soggy SPLAT!

I'll get you!

With an evil laugh he said,
'Take that! And that! And that!'
The shoe crashed down until the plate
Was smashed to smithereens
And a sticky, lumpy, splodgy mess
Was all that could be seen.

Billy heard no buzzing now
But he heard his mum come in
So picking up the evidence
He threw it in the bin.
But that night, as Billy slept,
His window open wide,
Ten thousand million million flies
Buzzed silently inside.
They hovered in their deadly swarm
Above young Billy's bed
And with a shout of 'Tally Ho!'
They flew right at his head!
Up his nose, inside his ears,
Across his sleeping eyes,
On his tongue and down his throat
They blocked up his insides.
No one heard him shout
And no one heard him cry
So just remember that
Next time you kill a fly.
And if, by chance, you do kill one
Then when you go to bed –
Make sure you close all windows
And cover up . . . your head!

Revenge of the Hamster

No one realized, nobody knew
The hamster was sleeping inside my dad's shoe.

He put in his foot and squashed flat its nose
So it opened its jaws and chomped on his toes.

While he was howling and hopping like mad
The hamster wreaked further revenge on my dad.

It scampered and scurried up his trouser leg . . .
And this time bit something much softer instead.

His eyes bulged and popped like marbles on stalks
And watered while he walked the strangest of walks.

His ears wiggled wildly while shooting out steam
All the dogs in the town heard his falsetto scream.

His face went deep purple, his hair stood on end,
His mouth like a letter box caught in the wind.

The hamster's revenge was almost complete . . .
Dad couldn't sit down for seventeen weeks.

Now dad doesn't give our hamster a chance . . .
He wears stainless-steel socks and metal underpants.

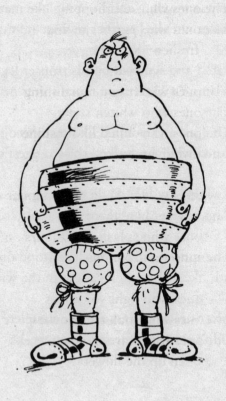

Invisible Magicians

Thanks be to all magicians,
The ones we never see,
Who toil away both night and day
Weaving spells for you and me.

The ones who paint the rainbows
The ones who salt the seas
The ones who purify the dew
And freshen up the breeze

The ones who brighten lightning
The ones who whiten snow
The ones who shine the sunshine
And give the moon its glow

The ones who buff the fluffy clouds
And powder blue the skies
The ones who splash the colours on
The sunset and sunrise

The ones who light volcanoes
The ones who soak the showers
The ones who wave the waves
And open up the flowers

The ones who spring the spring
And warm the summer air
The ones who carpet autumn
And frost the winter earth

The ones who polish icicles
The ones who scatter stars
The ones who cast their magic spells
Upon this world of ours

Thanks to one and thanks to all
Invisible and true
Nature's magic – heaven sent
To earth for me and you.

Pants Shape Poem

A hero's trunks are memorable, once seen they're not forgotten
They keep things under cover, like a superhero's bottom
The tighter and brighter the leather and lycra
The better remembered, the less to dislike – ah
Thongs are just wrong, you'd better not go there
Boxers and long johns – definitely no wear
Knickers and briefs just don't stand a chance
Because what you need are red underpants
Red underpants – big – red – underpants
You don't stand a chance without underpants
Red underpants are always fantastic
Except when they strain and
snap the elastic

Why Is a Bottom called a Bottom?

If the bottom of my body
Is that bit that's on the ground
Why is my bottom called my bottom
When it's only halfway down?

I Just Don't Trust the Furniture

I just don't trust the furniture
The desks have all got teeth
Grinning fangs inviting
Evilly delighting
At what they would be biting
And dragging down beneath . . .

Violet electric light
Bursts in violent blasts
Forked-tongue lightning slithers
Like vicious neon rivers
Everybody shivers
Until the storm has past

No one knows just how or why
But when they start to glow
When open lids are gaping
There is no escaping
The scratching and the scraping
Of the horrors down below

A gateway has been opened
A corridor unfurled
Its gravity commences
To hypnotize the senses
And drag you down defenceless
To its nightmare world

I just don't trust the furniture
The dark decaying smell
When hungry desks are humming
Their rumbling insides drumming
Something else is coming
Beware the chairs as well . . .

I just don't trust the furnit-urgh!

Me! I Teach PE

Me! I teach PE
Not history or geography, maths or English or RE
PE! That's me!
Not chemistry, biology, physics, drama, CDT
PE! That's me!
Not French or German, PSE or soci – poncy – ology
PE! That's me!

The subject of the gods – because it's taught by me
Bronzed and bold and beautiful – me! I teach PE!

Whatever the weather is weather for sports
Football pitch or tennis courts
All year round I wear my shorts
I write one sentence on reports

A mine of sporting general knowledge
Go on ask me who
Scored the winner in the FA Cup of seventy-two.
Who scored the only single try at Twickers eighty-three?
I'll tell you what and where and why cos me I teach PE

Watch *A Question of Sport* on BBC
PE! That's me!
The midweek match on ITV
PE! That's me!
Permanent action – B Sky B
PE! That's me!

I don't like fat kids, don't like weeds
Pigeon toes or knobbly knees
Kids in glasses, kids who wheeze
Do not give me wimps like these!

Sport's the only crucial thing
Numero Uno – that is me
PE Rules and I am King
The man in charge – I teach PE

It's great to teach this subject
I know I teach it well
It's great to teach a subject
That even I can spell . . .

P – E – That's me!

Down the Field

If anyone didn't know where Dad was
It was always 'try down the field'.
This could be anything from actually in the field
To in the greenhouse to feeding the chickens and livestock
To pottering in the shed
But it was always 'down the field'.

I suppose I always think of 'down the field'
As the clutter by the shed
That seems to have been there forever.
The brick pile and the bonfire site
Never seem to have reduced
In over twenty years
It's always looked like Steptoe's yard.

Greenhouses where I used to water tomatoes
For five pence an hour
Have been derelict and shattered
Since high winds stole the corrugated roof
From the big-shed extension
And spiralling it high in the air
Twisted it fifty yards or so
Shattering the wooden bone and glassy skin
The panes smithereened into shrapnel fallout,
Never the same after that.

Old cars, there's always been old cars.
Even as a youngster I can remember
Something wide and spacious,
Maybe a Zephyr or Humber
Weeds up to wheel arches
Ignition keys left in
It coughed and spluttered and very nearly started
But more importantly the radios crackled into life
And the horns worked perfectly.

Even now, these days,
It is something of a vehicle graveyard
As vans, caravans, two lorries
And even a bus rust in pieces.
The grey Massey Ferguson tractor,
The first thing I was ever allowed to drive alone,
The one Dad drove into the gatepost
The one whose mudguards we sat on
When Dad would drive it fast . . .
It can't have moved in those twenty years
And probably won't for twenty more.

'Down the field'
Has always somehow meant the same
And always somehow stayed the same.

And probably always will.

A selected list of titles available from Macmillan Children's Books

The prices shown below are correct at the time of going to press.
However, Macmillan Publishers reserves the right to show new retail prices
on covers, which may differ from those previously advertised.

The Works	ISBN-13: 978-0-330-48104-5	£6.99
	ISBN-10: 0-330-48104-5	
Give Us a Goal!	ISBN-13: 978-0-330-43654-0	£3.99
	ISBN-10: 0-330-43654-6	
How to Embarrass Teachers	ISBN-13: 978-0-330-44276-3	£3.99
	ISNB-10: 0-330-44276-7	
What Shape Is a Poem?	ISBN-13: 978-0-330-39707-0	£4.99
	ISBN-10: 0-330-39707-9	

All Pan Macmillan titles can be ordered from our website,
www.panmacmillan.com, or from your local bookshop
and are also available by post from:

Bookpost, PO Box 29, Douglas, Isle of Man IM99 1BQ
Credit cards accepted. For details:
Telephone: 01624 677237
Fax: 01624 670923
Email: bookshop@enterprise.net
www.bookpost.co.uk

Free postage and packing in the United Kingdom